M257 Unit 3
UNDERGRADUATE COMPUTING

Putting Java to work

Java in the large

Unit 3

This publication forms part of an Open University course M257 *Putting Java to work*. Details of this and other Open University courses can be obtained from the Student Registration and Enquiry Service, The Open University, PO Box 197, Milton Keynes MK7 6BJ, United Kingdom: tel. +44 (0)870 333 4340, email general-enquiries@open.ac.uk

Alternatively, you may visit the Open University website at http://www.open.ac.uk where you can learn more about the wide range of courses and packs offered at all levels by The Open University.

To purchase a selection of Open University course materials visit http://www.ouw.co.uk, or contact Open University Worldwide, Michael Young Building, Walton Hall, Milton Keynes MK7 6AA, United Kingdom for a brochure. tel. +44 (0)1908 858785; fax +44 (0)1908 858787; email ouwenq@open.ac.uk

The Open University
Walton Hall, Milton Keynes
MK7 6AA

First published 2007. Second edition 2008.

Edited, designed and typeset by The Open University.

Printed and bound in the United Kingdom by Hobbs the Printers Ltd.

ISBN 978 0 7492 6798 8

2.1

The paper used in this publication contains pulp sourced from forests independently certified to the Forest Stewardship Council® (FSC®) principles and criteria. Chain of custody certification allows the pulp from these forests to be tracked to the end use (see www.fsc-uk.org).

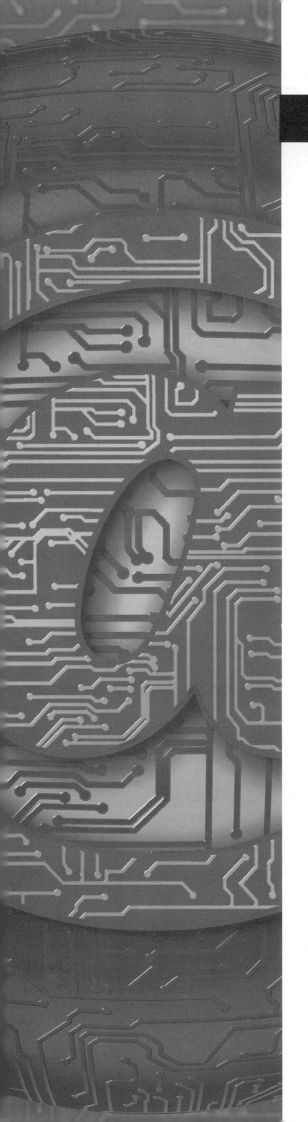

CONTENTS

M257 COURSE TEAM

M257 *Putting Java to work* was adapted from M254 *Java everywhere*.

M254 was produced by the following team.

Martin Smith, Course Team Chair and Author

Anton Dil, Author

Brendan Quinn, Author

Janet Van der Linden, Academic Editor

Barbara Poniatowska, Course Manager

Ralph Greenwell, Course Manager

Alkis Stavrinides, External Assessor, Coventry University

Critical readers

Pauline Curtis, Associate Lecturer

David Knowles, Associate Lecturer

Robin Walker, Associate Lecturer

Richard Walker, Associate Lecturer

The M257 adaptation was produced by:

Darrel Ince, Course Team Chair and Author

Richard Walker, Consultant Author and Critical Reader

Matthew Nelson, Critical Reader

Barbara Poniatowska, Course Manager

Ralph Greenwell, Course Manager

Alkis Stavrinides, External Assessor, Coventry University

Media development staff

Andrew Seddon, Media Project Manager

Garry Hammond, Editor

Ian Blackham, Editor

Anna Edgley-Smith, Editor

Jenny Brown, Freelance Editor

Andrew Whitehead, Designer and Graphic Artist

Glen Derby, Designer

Phillip Howe, Compositor

Lisa Hale, Compositor

Thanks are due to the Desktop Publishing Unit of the Faculty of Mathematics and Computing.

1 Introduction

The previous unit described the 'small' programming structures that languages such as Java offer. We have been concerned largely with how we store and operate on data, and how methods achieve their purposes. In this unit, we aim to show that Java is truly an object-oriented language. Object-oriented languages provide better support for what can be called 'programming in the large', a very different skill to the kind of programming of *Unit 2*.

The key object-oriented structure is the class, with its definitions of methods and variables. At the 'large' level, we are also able to describe relationships between classes, such as inheritance.

Programming in the large is about specifying how the parts of our programs should work with one another, and object-oriented languages provide us with keywords that allow us to reason about how methods may be used, how data may be manipulated and how objects may 'communicate' with one another.

Another key topic in this unit is the issue of how to create objects from class definitions, specifying the starting state of the objects in detail.

It is not difficult to write Java programs in a way resembling those of older, non object-oriented programming languages. However, to do this would miss the point and lose much of the power of the language. To derive the most from Java it is necessary to develop object-oriented code. By the end of this unit, you should be able to do this.

DeRemer and Kron (1976) called for 'a means to express intent regarding the overall program structure in a concise, precise and checkable form'.

2 Objects and classes

In this section, we begin to learn about object-oriented programming by looking at classes and objects. We see an example of how to write a class and examples of how to create objects.

2.1 Objects to model the world

Remember, from *Unit 1*, that an object is something that has a state: it has associated with it some variables whose values define that state. When we write programs, we have to decide which parts of the world we want to represent as objects in our programs. We also need to determine what aspects of their state we want to represent.

Here are some examples.

▶ A bank account could be modelled as an object whose state may be the name of the account holder, the current balance, the overdraft limit and a list of recent transactions.

▶ An aeroplane in an air-traffic control system could be modelled as an object; its state might consist of data that identifies the plane, its position and its eventual destination.

▶ A pull-down menu in the user interface of an applet may be modelled as an object; its state might consist of a list of the commands for the pull-down menu, the type of box that encloses the menu when it is on screen and its colour.

Another important feature of objects is that we can invoke methods on them. For example, the expression:

```
obj.setA(2);
```

has the interpretation that the method with name `setA` is invoked on the object `obj`.

An applet or application is a collection of communicating objects. The means of this communication is via methods, which allow data to be passed in to objects (by method arguments) and out of objects (as values returned by methods).

For example, assume that we have a simple word-processing application and a user wishes to count the number of words in a document. The user might pull down a menu that contains the 'word count' command, click on this command and see the word count displayed on the screen.

This seemingly simple piece of processing will contain considerable work 'behind the scenes' and would involve communication between a number of objects.

It might go as follows.

▶ The user interface object invokes a method of the pull-down menu object, resulting in the display of the pull-down menu.

▶ The pull-down menu object returns a value identifying that the user has selected the 'word count' command.

▶ The document object invokes a method to count the words in the document, with a count being incremented each time a word is found.

▶ A method is invoked on the window object, asking it to display the word count on the user's computer screen.

2.2 Defining classes and constructing objects

Once we have decided what kinds of objects we require in our system, we can describe them in general terms. Each category of objects we identify, such as 'bank account' or 'document', suggests a class of objects that share certain properties with one another.

A **class** is a definition of a category of objects. Having defined a class, we can **construct** objects using it, each object having its own state. Each category of objects in our system has a class definition.

Another word for 'construct' is 'instantiate'.

A class defines:

▶ the items of data that make up the state of an object, including their type: for example, whether they are integers, strings, or types defined by other classes;

▶ the 'behaviour' of objects of the class, by which we mean the methods that can be invoked on objects of the class.

Usually we maintain a reference to an object. When we invoke a method or access an instance variable, it is this reference we use with a dot notation. So, there are usually three steps to using an object and these are as follows.

1   Define a class.

2   Construct an object.

3   Store an object reference.

Step 1: defining a `User` class

Classes are like templates or blueprints for objects. They do not make objects, but they describe the features that objects of a class will have when created.

We will write the names of classes using a capital letter for each new word, following the convention used for Java's predefined classes.

By way of example, suppose that we have an applet and that we want to record how often users are accessing it. We want to define a class called `User` to model users of the applet. We wish to keep track of the user's identity (called `userID`) and email address (`emailAddress`), both of which can be represented as strings. We represent the number of times the applet has been visited as an integer, `numOfAccesses`. Below is a skeleton class definition for `User`, showing its instance variables:

```
public class User
{
    private String userID;
    private String emailAddress;
    private int numOfAccesses;

    // constructors have still to be written

    // methods have still to be written
}
```

The keyword `class` introduces the name of the class. We call this first line of the class the **class header**.

Inside the brackets, we define any instance variables, methods and constructors. The instance variables and methods of a class or object are known collectively as its **members**.

Remember that Java has two kinds of type: primitives and reference types. A class definition creates a **reference type** (we will also say **class type**). So, the class above defines a new reference type called `User`. Java provides many predefined class types.

Step 2: constructing a `User` object

In order to create an object you use the facility known as **construction**, which uses the keyword `new` together with a class name. For example, given our class `User`, the code:

```
new User()
```

The type of this expression is `User`.

results in an object of type `User` being created. We call this **invoking a constructor**.

Step 3: storing a reference to a `User` object

We saw in *Unit 2* that we could declare a reference variable by giving its type followed by an identifier. This requires a simple statement of the form:

```
ClassName objectName;
```

where `ClassName` is the name of a class (either one we defined or one in a Java library, such as `String`) and `objectName` is an identifier.

Any such declaration creates a **reference variable**. In the example above, the type of the reference variable `objectName` is `ClassName`. To create a reference of type `User`, we would write something like:

```
User john;
```

In order to store a reference to an actual object in such a reference variable, we need to assign a value to the variable. This is usually done by assigning a newly constructed object as follows:

```
john = new User();
```

Figure 1 shows the relationship between a reference variable and an object. Each object has its own copies of any instance variables.

When a variable is created it is given a default value; Figure 1 shows this. For references the default is null, while for other types it depends on the type – for example, for integers it is zero.

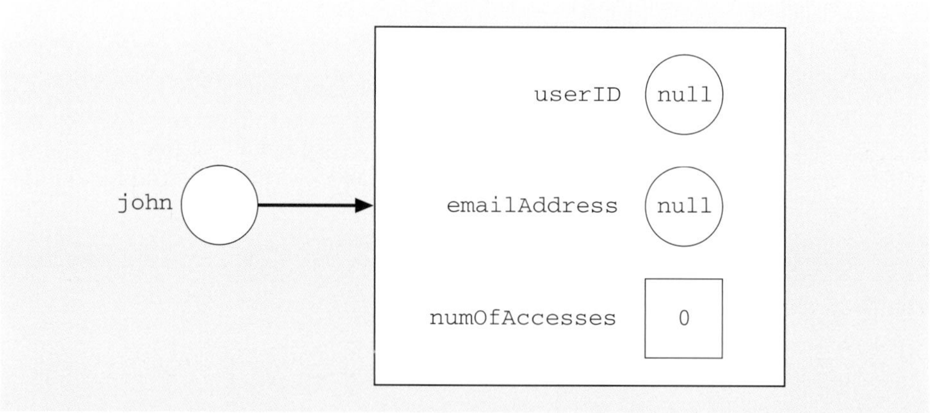

Figure 1   After executing `john = new User()`

We have represented the `userID` and `emailAddress` containers as circles to emphasize that they are themselves reference variables. Neither of these variables currently references an object, which is indicated by their value being `null`.

Combining declaration, construction and assignment

The three steps outlined above can be written on one line of code. For example, creation of an object of type `User` and storing of a reference to it in variable `john` could have been written as follows:

```
User john = new User();
```

The keyword `null`

The literal `null` represents a reference that does not point at any object. This is the only literal for reference types and any instance reference variable that has not been initialized will have this value by default. Because it is a literal, it is also possible to assign the value `null` to a reference variable. For example, we could write:

```
User jane = null;
```

We shall see more about these topics in Section 4.

2.3 Reference variables and assignment

The reference `jane` can at any time be made to refer to an object, for example by using a `User` constructor and the keyword `new`:

```
jane = new User();
```

As the reference `john` is of the same type, referring to a `User` object, we could also write:

```
jane = john;
```

The relationship between `jane` and `john` after this last statement is illustrated in Figure 2 (below).

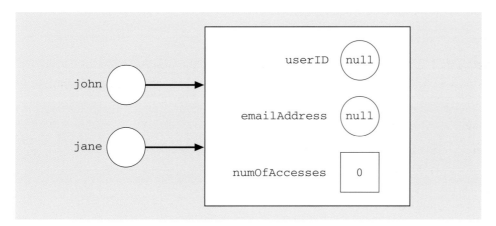

Figure 2   After executing `jane = john;`

Now suppose we make the `userID` variable in this object reference the string `"Bridgend"`. (This could be done by assignment to `userID`, via a method.)

This would mean that the `userID` variable in the object referenced by `john` and `jane` references the string `"Bridgend"`, since `john` and `jane` refer to the same object. The result is illustrated in Figure 3.

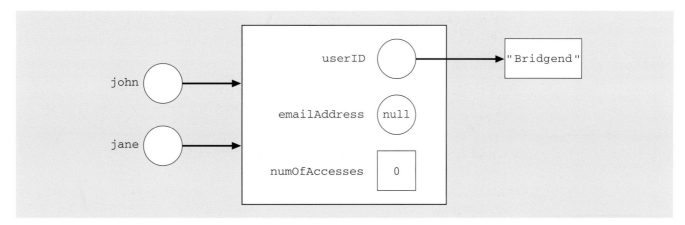

Figure 3   Variables `john` and `jane` referencing the same object

Any changes to the state of an object affect the execution of code involving any of the object references.

Here we are using a constructor with two arguments. Section 4 explains this in detail.

If we require two objects with the same contents we should instead have written something like the following:

```
User emma = new User("Cornes", "cornee@joke.com");
User maria = new User("Cornes", "cornee@joke.com");
```

In this case, changes made to one object would have no effect on the other object. This is illustrated in Figure 4.

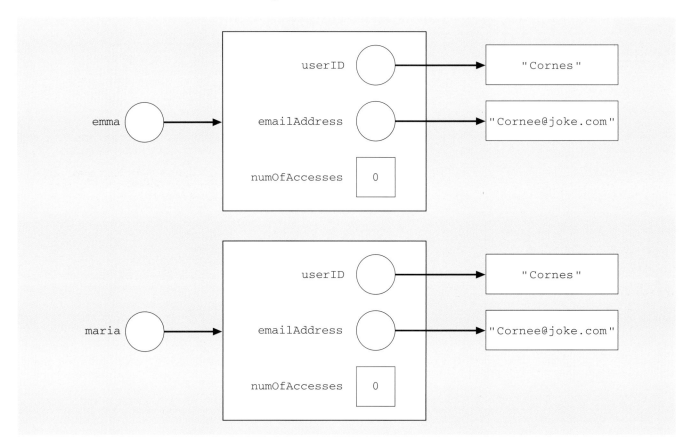

Figure 4   Variables **emma** and **maria** referencing different objects

Arrays of references

You can also declare an array of users, for example:

```
User[] users = new User[10];
```

This would result in there being ten locations, each capable of holding a `User` reference. By default, each of these locations would have the value `null`, initially. You could make the first location reference an object as follows:

```
users[0] = new User();
```

and other locations could be initialized in a similar way.

3 Information hiding

A class is used to define objects, and is therefore a key concept in Java and in object-oriented languages in general. In this section we look in more detail at how we write classes and how we can write code that is likely to be easy to use and maintain.

3.1 Getter and setter methods

It can be useful to classify methods according to the kinds of work that they do. Two important kinds are known as 'getters' and 'setters'.

A **getter method** (also called an 'accessor' method) is one that accesses some attribute of an object. A getter method should not change the state of the object.

To ensure that these methods are easily identified, we will follow the popular convention of beginning their names with the word 'get'. It is normal to follow this with the name of the instance variable whose value we are accessing.

The language does not enforce this naming convention.

A **setter method** (also called a 'mutator' method) is one that changes the state of an object by setting the value of an instance variable. Setter methods do not normally return a value.

We will follow the convention that this kind of method will have a name beginning with the word 'set'. It is normal to follow this with the name of the attribute whose value is being set.

These methods are often the first we write for a class. There are no keywords in the language to create them; we just use naming conventions to help identify them.

Getter and setter methods for the `User` class

Recall that the `User` class describes a user of an applet, and that we wish to store information about the user's ID, email address and how many times he or she has accessed the applet.

Suppose that we require getter methods for each of the three instance variables defined in `User`, and setters for only its `String` variables. In addition, we need a method that updates the number of times the user has accessed the applet.

We can now fill in more of the detail of this class:

```java
public class User
{
    private String userID;
    private String emailAddress;
    private int numOfAccesses;

    // constructors have still to be written

    // setter methods
    public void setUserID (String usIdVal)
    {
        userID = usIdVal;
    }

    public void setEmailAddress (String emailAddressVal)
    {
        emailAddress = emailAddressVal;
    }

    // getter methods
    public String getUserID ()
    {
        return userID;
    }

    public String getEmailAddress ()
    {
        return emailAddress;
    }

    public int getNumOfAccesses ()
    {
        return numOfAccesses;
    }

    // update number of accesses by this user
    public void updateNumOfAccesses ()
    {
        numOfAccesses++;
    }
}
```

The code for the methods in the class is straightforward, the only slightly complicated aspect being the use of the `return` statement, which terminates a method and passes a value back to the object that invoked the method. The type of the value returned is indicated in the method header. For example, `getUserID` declares that it returns a `String`.

Next we look at how we can make use of objects of the `User` class.

3.2 Member access by dot notation

Having defined the class User, we can construct objects of that class and access its members via a dot notation with an object reference, provided we have indicated that this access is to be allowed.

The keyword public in front of a member in the class User indicates that it may be accessed using dot notation with a User reference variable. In contrast, because we have used the keyword private in front of the User instance variables, there is no access outside the class itself to these variables.

For example, if john references a User object we may not write:

```
john.numOfAccesses = -1; // not allowed
```

But, because the updateNumOfAccesses method is public, we may write:

```
john.updateNumOfAccesses(); // allowed
```

to increment the instance variable numOfAccesses in the object referenced by john.

Notice that we did *not* provide a setter method for numOfAccesses, which would have looked like this:

```
public void setNumOfAccesses (int n)
{
    numOfAccesses = n;
}
```

We did not do this because it would allow the same kind of undesirable access (via a method) to the numOfAccesses variable. We have made use of information hiding to ensure that programmers who employ this class can rely on methods to perform their required tasks. A programmer is not allowed to know how data is stored and cannot directly manipulate the data except under very strict rules through the methods.

Separation of concerns

Of course, setter and getter methods are only the simplest methods we tend to have in our classes, so let us look at some other methods we might have.

Let us assume that the application of which the User class is a part requires a method that checks whether a user has made any accesses before. We call this method zeroAccesses: it returns a true value if the user has made no accesses and a false value if he or she has made at least one access.

```
public boolean zeroAccesses ()
{
    return (numOfAccesses == 0);
}
```

Furthermore, let us also assume that there is a need for a method that compares the user's ID and email address, to see if they are the same. The method returns a true value if the two strings are the same and a false value otherwise.

```
public boolean isEmailUserID ()
{
    return userID.equals(emailAddress);
}
```

Activity 3.1
Experimenting with the User **class.**

This method makes use of the `equals` method of `String` objects and returns `true` if the strings referenced by `userId` and `emailAddress` have the same contents, within the receiving object.

We aim to have classes model one kind of object and to have each method deal with one small job, so that it is clear to which class and to which part of the class we should look when we have a particular aim to achieve. We call this **separation of concerns**. This is one of the motivations for having separate setter and getter methods.

Compilation and run-time errors with `null`

At compile time you may receive a warning that a local reference variable has not been initialized. You might be tempted at this point to assign the reference variable `null` to satisfy the compiler that it has been assigned a value, but this is often a mistake. Ask yourself, instead, if the variable is required, or if it should be made to reference some object.

'Pointer' is another name for reference.

The error may not become apparent until run time, when you may have a program crash with what is known as a `NullPointerException`. This means that somewhere in your code you have used a reference thinking that it referred to an object, but the reference had the value `null`.

SAQ 1

Write a class called `Chef` that has instance variables for the chef's name, the name of the chef's signature dish, the price of that dish in pence, and whether or not the chef does home catering. Choose an appropriate type for each variable and provide setter and getter methods for each.

ANSWER..

The following types are reasonable choices for the four identified instance variables: the names of the chef and the signature dish can be strings, the price of the dish in pence calls for an integer type, and the information about whether or not home catering is provided may be represented by a boolean (true or false) value. It would be possible to have the price of a dish as a floating-point number, but this would introduce inaccuracies due to approximations associated with these types, and the question specified price in pence, so a floating-point type was not required.

The following class is suggested:

```java
public class Chef
{
    // we choose appropriate instance variable names
    private String name, signatureDish;
    private int signaturePrice;
    private boolean homeCaters;

    // setter methods
    public void setName (String aName)
    {
        name = aName;
    }

    public void setSignatureDish (String aDish)
    {
        signatureDish = aDish;
    }

    public void setSignaturePrice (int aPrice)
    {
        signaturePrice = aPrice;
    }

    public void setHomeCaters (boolean willCater)
    {
        homeCaters = willCater;
    }

    // getter methods
    public String getName ()
    {
        return name;
    }

    public String getSignatureDish ()
    {
        return signatureDish;
    }

    public int getSignaturePrice ()
    {
        return signaturePrice;
    }

    public boolean getHomeCaters ()
    {
        return homeCaters;
    }
}
```

3.3   Packages

Some languages call a package a 'library', which is another name for a collection of related classes.

Large programs are built up from a number of classes working together in concert. There is a program structure known as the **package**, used to associate a number of classes that are closely related to one another. In other words, if classes form a cohesive group, they should be marked as belonging to the same package. For example, Java has a collection of classes named `java.math`, which contains two classes called `BigDecimal` and `BigInteger`. These two classes contain instance variables and methods for doing arithmetic with large numbers and having them in the same package is a useful way of grouping them.

If we wanted to make use of this package, we would add a statement to advise the Java system of this, by adding an `import` statement at the beginning of our program. In this case we would say:

The .* notation means 'all the classes in the package'.

```
import java.math.*;
public class User
{
    // etc.
}
```

to indicate that we want to use all the classes in the `java.math` package within our class `User`.

You will see other useful packages the language has to offer later in the course.

3.4   Access modifiers

One of the key refinements of our object-oriented programming skills in this unit is learning how we can specify that only certain classes of objects may invoke a method and only certain classes may access an instance variable.

There are two kinds of access to class members: qualified or simple, using what we call a **qualified name** or a **simple name**. A name used with an object reference and a dot notation is a qualified name, for example `john.getNumOfAccesses()`; a name without a reference and dot notation is a simple name, for example `getNumOfAccesses()`.

Inheritance and member accessibility

If we say a member is **inherited** we mean that the subclass has the same access to it as if it were defined in the subclass. It can be accessed using its simple name. This kind of access is available only via an inheritance relationship. Any other class would have to have a reference to an object, and use a qualified name.

It is useful to be able to create different levels of information hiding, allowing us to share information between certain classes and deny other classes access to details they should not and do not need to know.

The classes that you have seen in the course so far were all constructed in such a way that the instance variables have been `private` and therefore have not been available for access outside their class, but the methods have been `public` and therefore have been available to be accessed. This is generally best programming practice. However, there are circumstances when other levels of access should be allowed.

There are three keywords associated with controlling levels of access to class members in Java: `public`, `protected` and `private`. These are known as **access modifiers**. However, there is actually a fourth level of access, 'default'. There is no 'default' keyword; default access arises when none of the access modifiers is specified.

The most accessible (least restrictive) level is public, followed by protected, default and then private. This means that if you fail to specify an access level, by default you get a fairly restricted access to class methods and instance variables. Only the private access level is more restrictive.

In the following sections we will look at variations on how we might declare members of the `User` class, the effect this has on whether classes can access the members of `User` objects and also which members of the `User` class would be inherited by any of its subclasses.

3.4.1 The `public` access level

If you precede an instance variable or a method of a `public` class with the keyword `public`, then any class can access that member using a reference and a dot notation (that is, using a qualified name). For example, consider the class:

```
package AppletUser;
public class UserV2
{
    // public instance variable
    public int numOfAccesses;

    // public setter method
    public void setNumOfAccesses (int n)
    {
        numOfAccesses = n;
    }
}
```

If class `TestUserV2` creates an object of this class, it can also have statements that use qualified names to access the object's members:

```
import AppletUser.*;
public class TestUserV2
{
    public static void main (String[] args)
    {
        // this method has a UserV2 reference
        UserV2 myUser;

        // once initialized, the reference can be used
        // to access members of a UserV2 object
        myUser = new UserV2();

        // qualified access to instance variable numOfAccesses
        myUser.numOfAccesses = 1;

        // qualified access to setNumOfAccesses method
        myUser.setNumOfAccesses(1);
    }
}
```

This is allowed because both of these members were declared to be `public`.

Inheritance of `public` members

Any `public` members are inherited by all subclasses, so they can be accessed within those classes without a dot notation. For example, a class extending `UserV2` could have statements using simple names:

```
import AppletUser.*;
public class MyUser extends UserV2
{
    public void doThings ()
    {
        // simple name access to numOfAccesses variable
        numOfAccesses = 1;

        // simple name access to setNumOfAccesses method
        setNumOfAccesses(1); // same effect as line above
    }
}
```

3.4.2 The `protected` and default access levels

Qualified name access to members designated `protected` or of default access level (because they have no access modifier) is available only to classes in the same package. In this respect, there is no distinction between these two access levels.

For example, if we have:

```
package AppletUser;
public class UserV3
{
    // protected instance variable
    protected int numOfAccesses;

    // default access level method
    void setNumOfAccesses (int n)
    {
        numOfAccesses = n;
    }
}
```

and we were to test the class as follows:

```
import AppletUser.*; // this class does not compile!
public class TestUserV3
{
    public static void main (String[] args)
    {
        // this method has a UserV3 reference
        UserV3 myUser;

        // initialize the reference
        myUser = new UserV3();

        // qualified access to instance variable numOfAccesses
        // is not allowed!
        myUser.numOfAccesses = 1;

        // qualified access to setNumOfAccesses method
        // is not allowed!
        myUser.setNumOfAccesses(1);
    }
}
```

we would find that the class `TestUserV3` does not compile, because the condition that it should be in the same package as `UserV3` is not satisfied and therefore it cannot access either the protected or the default access level members of `UserV3`. Instead of importing the classes in the `AppletUser` package, the `TestUserV3` class would have to be preceded by the words `package AppletUser;`

Inheritance of **`protected`** and default members

Where the protected and default access levels differ is in terms of inheritance of members by subclasses.

Any subclass inherits any protected and public members of its superclass.

Any subclass in the same package as its superclass inherits not only the protected and public members of its superclass, but also any default access level members. Default access level is sometimes known as 'package access' for this reason.

Thus the default access type is more restrictive in terms of inheritance of members than the protected type. These members are inherited only by subclasses in the same package as the superclass.

For example, the class `UserV3` above has the method `setNumOfAccesses` defined as *default* access level. Therefore, any class extending `UserV3` and intending to use `setNumOfAccesses` must be preceded by the statement:

```
package AppletUser;
```

instead of importing from the `AppletUser` package.

If `setNumOfAccesses` had been defined with protected access level, then it would have been sufficient for any subclass definition to start with an import statement.

3.4.3 The `private` access level

By prefacing a method or instance variable with the keyword `private` the programmer specifies that the member can be accessed only within its defining class. This is the most restrictive level of access you can specify.

Private members are never inherited, so can never be accessed by subclasses as if they were part of the subclass.

Which access level should I use?

The various levels of access we have described here can be mixed throughout a class definition. In keeping with the principles of information hiding, it is generally best to use the most restrictive level of access that meets your purpose. Using a more accessible level than is necessary is liable to cause maintenance problems, if not actual misuse, eventually.

A rule of thumb is to have `public` methods and `private` data. The premise of this rule is that the methods are the channels of communication with the object, which you wish to keep open, and that the data is the object's internal representation of information, not for outside viewing.

Most of the Java classes that you will encounter will have most, if not all, of their methods declared as `public` and their instance variables declared as `private`. Some methods may provide a service needed only inside the class. These are often known as **helper methods** or helpers and it is normal practice for them to be `private`.

We will not be making extensive use of protected or default access types, but your understanding of Java would be incomplete without us having discussed them. A common error is to forget to use an access modifier, at which point, if your classes are not in the same package, you may find that your code does not compile.

3.4.4 Inheritance and protected members

Since private members are not inherited, a subclass cannot make direct use of them. For this reason, some guides recommend using protected access for instance variables in the case that the class is likely to be extended. Since protected members are inherited, this strategy provides more flexibility for a subclass to implement methods.

SAQ 2

(a) Why would you use `private` instance variables and `public` methods in a class?

(b) What level of access to a member would you expect if you did not use one of the modifiers `private`, `public` or `protected`?

(c) In what situation would you be likely to use a `private` method?

ANSWERS ....

(a) You would do this to assist in information hiding: the details of how data is stored are hidden from outside classes and the class will take responsibility for modifying and accessing the state of an object via methods.

(b) This would result in the level of access known as 'default'. Only classes in the same package as the class in which the default access members appear will have access to those members.

(c) If you did not want the method to be available for access outside the class, but you required a method to perform some internal processing within the class, or such a method made your code easier to use or maintain.

3.5   Static variables and static methods

So far, we have talked about each object having its own data and methods, and we have invoked methods on individual objects. This is the normal situation, but there may be occasions when we want to share an item of data between objects.

There is another type of variable called a **static variable**, also known as a **class variable**. When you declare a static variable in a class, you are specifying that there is exactly one copy of the variable for all objects defined by that class. The name 'class variable' reflects that the variable is created once for the whole class and not individually for the objects of that class. You may find it useful to think of it as a class-wide variable.

Static variables and methods are both introduced by means of the keyword `static`, which is another example of a modifier.

Let us add to our example a new static variable, `totalAccesses`, and two related methods:

```
public class User
{
    private int numOfAccesses;
    // static (class) variable declaration
    private static int totalAccesses;

    public void updateNumOfAccesses ()
    {
        numOfAccesses++;
    }

    public int getNumOfAccesses ()
    {
        return numOfAccesses;
    }

    public void updateTotalAccesses ()
    {
        totalAccesses++;
    }

    public int getTotalAccesses ()
    {
        return totalAccesses;
    }
    // and other methods
}
```

Notice that we added the word `static` after the word `private`, so that we provided further information about the kind of variable `totalAccesses` is. Consider the following test class:

The order of the modifiers `static` and `private` is not significant.

```
public class TestUser
{
    public static void main (String[] args)
    {
        // this method has two User references
        User uOne, uTwo;

        // once initialized, the references can be used
        // to access members of the User objects they
        // reference
        uOne = new User();
        uTwo = new User();

        uOne.updateNumOfAccesses();
        uOne.updateTotalAccesses();
        uTwo.updateTotalAccesses();

        System.out.println(uOne.getNumOfAccesses());
        System.out.println(uTwo.getNumOfAccesses());
        System.out.println(uOne.getTotalAccesses());
        System.out.println(uTwo.getTotalAccesses());
    }
}
```

Bearing in mind that the integer instance variables in our `User` objects are initialized to zero by default, the output of the `TestUser` program would be:

```
1
0
2
2
```

This is because there is an instance of `numOfAccesses` for each object of the class `User` we make, so any changes to the value of this variable are made only in the object that makes them; however, there is only one copy of `totalAccesses` for all objects of the class, so any changes to this variable are seen in all objects of the class.

3.6 | Static variables and their uses

Static members are unusual in that they exist without you creating an object of the class. They have a limited number of correct uses. You should not be tempted to use them as a way of avoiding constructing objects.

Constants

A common use is to define some constant associated with the class. For example, the Java package associated with mathematical processing implements the mathematical constant `PI` in this way.

Pi is the name of the Greek character π, used for the constant ratio of a circle's circumference to its diameter.

One value for all objects

A second use of class variables and methods is to implement data that has only one value for every object of that class. One common example of this is to keep count of the number of objects of a class type that have been created. It might lead to errors if each object kept its own version of this count, as each object would have to update the count every time a new object came into existence and it would be easy to forget to update some object's copy of this variable.

3.7 | Dot notation for static variables

Suppose that class `User` has a public static variable `day`, recording the day of the week as an integer:

```
public class User
{
    public static int day;
    // etc.
}
```

This could be used to ensure that all objects of the class `User` record the same value for the day of the week.

We can create an object of type `User` referenced by `jane`:

```
User jane = new User();
```

However, to access `day` it is preferable to write `User.day` rather than `jane.day`, as the latter suggests instance data.

3.8 Static methods and their uses

Static (that is, class) methods are also specified using the modifier `static`.

Static methods are allowed only simple name access to static (not instance) variables. One typical use of a static method would occur with the scenario described previously, where a class variable describes the number of objects of the class that have been created. A static method could be used to increment this counter.

> If you try to access a non-static variable from a static method then you will get a syntax error.

You will also find static methods in the Java libraries, where they carry out general functions not associated with objects. For example, the static method `max` within the class `Math` returns the greater of its two arguments. The method header for one version of `max` looks like this:

```
public static double max (double a, double b)
```

Thus the code:

```
double val = Math.max (Math.PI, 4.0);
```

determines the greater of its two arguments and places the result within the double variable `val`.

The **main** method

Remember that when we write executable programs we always have a `main` method, which is where the execution of the program begins. You will have seen a header that looks similar to this:

> The `main` method is the starting point for the execution of a Java program.

```
public static void main (String[] args)
{
    // main code
}
```

3.9 Declaring constants: the keyword **final**

Most languages have a way of stating that a value cannot be changed. In Java, it is the keyword `final`. When you precede an identifier name with the word `final`, it means that once its value is specified, nothing in your code can change (or attempt to change) its value. Thus the declaration:

```
static final int MAX_VALUE = 12;
```

declares a constant `MAX_VALUE` with the value `12`. We will adopt the convention that identifiers for constants are written in upper-case letters, with words separated by an underscore character.

The constant `MAX_VALUE` is a class variable, because it is declared using the keyword `static`. It is common for constants to be static, because many such values are 'universal' (for example, the speed of light, or the value of pi) and it would not make sense for objects to be able to decide the value themselves.

> A `final` reference variable will always refer to the same object, but the state of that object can be changed.

The example of `PI`, the ratio of a circle's circumference to its diameter, also uses `final`. In the `Math` class you will find:

```
public static final double PI = 3.14159265358979323846;
```

It makes sense that `PI` is all of these things. It is `public` because we wish it to be available to other classes, it is `static` because it has one value for all objects of the class, and it is `final` because pi is a constant. It is `double` because that is the most accurate decimal representation we can use.

> Modifiers may be in any order, but it is important to stick to one order for consistency.

4   Constructors

When an object is created, it will have a particular starting state. In this section we discuss the issues involved in specifying this starting state and the Java techniques available to do so.

4.1   Controlling the initial state of objects

In order to specify the initial state of an object when it is constructed, we can use a **constructor**. A constructor is a piece of code that contains instructions on how to initialize objects of a class. We can write our own constructors so that we can control how objects are initialized.

A constructor must have the same name as its class. In this section we use a simple example, the class `Coordinate`. We show this class with an example `public` access level constructor below:

```
public class Coordinate
{
    // instance variables
    private int xPos, yPos;

    // a public Coordinate constructor
    public Coordinate (int xVal, int yVal)
    {
        xPos = xVal;
        yPos = yVal;
    }

    // methods of the class
}
```

In this example the constructor has two arguments, which are used to pass initial values of the two `Coordinate` instance variables.

A constructor creates an object when you invoke it using the keyword `new`. For example, the code:

```
new Coordinate(2, 2)
```

creates a new object described by the class `Coordinate` and sets each of its instance variables to the value 2. The types and order of any arguments in such an expression must match those of the arguments of some constructor for the class, just as for a method invocation.

To store a reference to a `Coordinate` object in a reference `newCoord` we could write a line like the following example:

```
Coordinate newCoord = new Coordinate(20, -2)
```

Although constructors look like methods, according to the language specification they are not. One notable difference is that the code for the constructor does not declare a returned type. The type it returns in this case is actually `Coordinate`, but we do not write this in the constructor header. If we were to write a return type, such as `void` or `int`, the compiler would interpret the code as being a method.

4.2 The steps in construction

There are actually three steps involved in constructing an object.

1   An 'empty' (default) object is created.

2   Any explicit initialization (outside the constructor) is performed.

3   The constructor code is executed.

In step 1 instance variables are initialized to default values, which are

▶   `null` for all reference types

▶   `false` for `booleans` and

▶   0 for numeric types (to their respective precisions)

▶   `'\u0000'` for the char type (the first Unicode value, which is equivalent to the integer value 0).

4.3 Explicit initializers

Step 2 of construction takes into account any explicit initializing expressions for instance variables, examples of which are shown below:

```
public class Coordinate
{
    // explicit initialization of instance variables
    private int xPos = 100;
    private int yPos = 200;

    // a Coordinate constructor
    public Coordinate (int xVal, int yVal)
    {
        xPos = xVal;
        yPos = yVal;
    }

    // methods of the class
}
```

In this case, when the given `Coordinate` constructor is invoked, after the empty object is created, the explicit initialization is performed. In our example the variables `xPos` and `yPos` would start with the default value 0, but after explicit initialization they would have the values 100 and 200. These values would be overwritten by any initialization performed by the constructor code in step 3. Therefore, if we write:

```
Coordinate newCoord = new Coordinate(2, 2);
```

we still create an object described by the class `Coordinate` and set its two instance variables to the value 2.

In general it is best to perform initialization of instance data within a constructor, rather than using explicit initialization. This makes it easy to locate the code where initialization takes place.

4.4   Writing your own constructors

Often when you are writing classes, you will provide a number of constructors, catering for a selection of initialization possibilities. Each constructor must have a unique set of arguments (if any). For example, the code for the class `Coordinate` shown below contains three constructors.

```
public class Coordinate
{
    private int xPos, yPos;
    private static final int DEFAULT_X = 0;
    private static final int DEFAULT_Y = 0;

    // two-argument constructor
    public Coordinate (int xVal, int yVal)
    {
        xPos = xVal;
        yPos = yVal;
    }

    // one-argument constructor
    public Coordinate (int xVal)
    {
     xPos = xVal;
     yPos = DEFAULT_Y;
    }

    // zero-argument constructor
    public Coordinate ()
    {
     xPos = DEFAULT_X;
     yPos = DEFAULT_Y;
    }

    // methods of the class
}
```

It is good practice to set all instance variables to some value, however many arguments the constructor has. Above, we have used constants to define default initial values for the instance variables of the class when the user has not provided values.

Here are some more examples of classes and constructors.

Example 1

Consider a class that is used to store details about voters. The class defines an `age` instance variable. We will write a zero-argument constructor to create a voter with default `age` and a one-argument constructor to set the voter's `age` to an integer value.

```
public class Voter
{
    private int age;
    private final static int MINIMUM_AGE = 18;

    // a one-argument constructor
    public Voter (int personAge)
    {
        age = personAge;
    }

    // a zero-argument constructor
    public Voter ()
```

```
        {
            age = MINIMUM_AGE;
        }

        // methods...
    }
```

We used a `final static` constant here to create a default `age`. Any object created using the zero-argument constructor would initially have its `age` variable set to this value. The one-argument constructor allows the programmer to specify the initial value of the `age` variable.

It may not be desirable to provide a zero-argument constructor as we did above. We may not want to allow a `Voter` to be constructed if the programmer cannot provide the voter's age. It may also be desirable to have the one-argument constructor perform a test to ensure that the age it receives as an argument is greater than or equal to the minimum age.

One topic we have not tackled is how to initialize reference variables in our constructors, so we look at this case next.

Example 2

Suppose we want to write a zero-argument constructor for the `User` class. Since we have no values passed as arguments we might choose to use empty strings for the user ID and email address, while setting the number of accesses to zero:

```
    public User ()
    {
        numOfAccesses = 0;
        userID = "";              // empty strings
        emailAddress = "";
    }
```

This would allow us to create an object using a zero-argument constructor as follows:

```
    User livingstone = new User();
```

The `emailAddress` and `userID` variables would both reference empty strings. This would limit how much you could do with these values: for example, you could not send an email to the stored address.

We could also have written something like this for our zero-argument constructor:

```
    public User ()
    {
        numOfAccesses = 0;
        userID = null;
        emailAddress = null;
    }
```

If we had done this, then the following code would have caused a crash:

This is a `NullPointerException` again.

```
    User george = new User();
    String e = george.getEmailAddress();
    System.out.println(e.charAt(0));
```

This is because there is no object on which the `charAt` method can be invoked in this case, since `george.getEmailAddress()` returns `null`.

Another possibility is to use some default text (which could be stored in `String` constants, but is shown using literals here):

```
public User ()
{
    numOfAccesses = 0;
    emailAddress = "lostmail@home.com";
    userID = "unknownID";
}
```

Now the code that previously caused an error would run, although it might not behave quite as we expect, depending on how we use the information.

Clearly we need to think carefully about what values we assign to reference variables when writing constructors. Possibly we should not have defined a zero-argument constructor at all, so that a programmer wanting to create a `User` object is forced to provide necessary information.

Constructor access level

We have created all our constructors as `public` because it is usual that we want to create objects from outside the class in which we define them. However, we can make it illegal to create objects of the type outside the defining class by making the constructor `private`. For example, you cannot create an object of the `Math` class because its only constructor is `private`. Constructors can also be given `protected` or default access level.

Inheritance of constructors

Constructors are not considered class members and are not inherited.

SAQ 3

What three steps take place when a constructor is called?

ANSWER...

1   An object is created with default values for its variables.

2   Any explicit initialization outside the constructor is performed.

3   The constructor code is executed.

SAQ 4

Recall the class `Chef`, given earlier in answer to SAQ 1. The relevant part of the class is shown below:

```
public class Chef
{
    private String name, signatureDish;
    private int signaturePrice;
    private boolean homeCaters;
}
```

(a) Show how you would create an object of this class, referenced by an identifier `pierrePoisson`, assuming that you have a zero-argument constructor.

(b) Assume that the zero-argument constructor does not perform any initialization, and that getter methods are provided in the class `Chef` (as given in SAQ 1) for all its variables. After part (a), what values would you expect the following expressions to return?

```
pierrePoisson.getSignaturePrice();
pierrePoisson.getName();
pierrePoisson.getName().equals("true");
```

(c) Show how you would create an object of class `Chef`, referenced by `peterBeck`, assuming the existence of a four-argument `Chef` constructor with a header `public Chef(String chefName, String dishName, int price, boolean caters);` The name of the chef is Peter Beck and his signature dish is bacon, priced at £3.30. (The `signaturePrice` is represented in pence.) He does home catering.

(d) What values would you expect the following expressions to produce after making `peterBeck` reference the object suggested in part (c)?

```
System.out.println(peterBeck.getSignaturePrice());
System.out.println(peterBeck.getName());
System.out.println(peterBeck.getName().equals("true"));
```

ANSWERS ....

(a) `Chef pierrePoisson = new Chef();`

(b) The first two expressions would return `0` and `null` (not the string `"null"`, there is no `String` object). The third expression would cause the program to crash with a null pointer exception.

(c) The order of arguments in your answer should match the constructor.

```
Chef peterBeck = new Chef("Peter Beck", "bacon", 330, true);
```

Notice that we had to convert the pounds and pence price into an integer pence value.

(d) We would expect the following output:

```
330
Peter Beck
false
```

4.5 The default constructor

You may be wondering how we have managed to construct objects thus far, given that we have not been writing constructors. The answer is that if you do not write a constructor for your class, Java kindly provides you with one. This special constructor is called the **default constructor** and it has no arguments. You will not see this constructor appear in your class, but you may assume that it is present, if you do not write any constructors of your own.

In order to understand this better, we first need to explain the use of the keywords `this` and `super` in the context of constructors.

The keyword `this`

The word `this` can be used to invoke a constructor. You can think of `this` as a reference to the class in which it appears.

For example, if the Java interpreter encounters the statement:

```
this(1000, 300);
```

as the *first statement* in a constructor `ClassName()`, it will look for a matching `ClassName` constructor with two arguments. When that `ClassName` constructor is invoked, the three-step construction procedure is followed as before.

For example, consider the code shown below, which contains the skeletal description of `ThreeInt`. The class has three instance variables `p`, `q` and `r` and four constructors. The variables are not accessible to other classes, as we have declared them to be `private`.

```java
public class ThreeInt
{
    private int p, q, r;

    public ThreeInt ()
    {
        this(0, 0, 0);
    }

    public ThreeInt (int a)
    {
        this(a, 0, 0);
    }

    public ThreeInt (int a, int b)
    {
        this(a, b, 0);
    }

    public ThreeInt (int a, int b, int c)
    {
        p = a; q = b; r = c;
    }

    // methods associated with ThreeInt
}
```

The first three constructors make use of the three-argument constructor. This is a way of reusing constructors you have written and can assist with readability when you have several constructors.

Do not think of `this(a, b, 0)` as a call to a method. It is only possible to invoke constructors in this way in this context: from another constructor, and then you must do so at the beginning of the constructor. (Other code may appear after the constructor invocation.) This is another significant difference between constructors and methods.

In addition, a constructor cannot invoke itself (whereas a method can). This helps to ensure that objects are correctly initialized. For example, the following 'cyclic' code is illegal:

```java
public ThreeInt ()
{
    this();
}
```

The keyword **super**

Assume that we want to extend the class `ThreeInt` presented earlier, by adding a further integer instance variable and a few other methods.

```
public class FourInt extends ThreeInt
{
    private int s;
    // methods
}
```

Now we would want to ensure correct initialization of the instance variables p, q and r defined in `ThreeInt`, but we would have to rely on `ThreeInt` to do this, as the data is `private`.

Some code for a constructor in `FourInt` that would do this is shown below:

```
public FourInt (int a, int b, int c, int d)
{
    super(a, b, c);
    s = d;
}
```

The code `super(a, b, c)` results in the three-argument constructor of `ThreeInt` being executed, which results in the values of a, b and c being assigned to the instance variables p, q and r associated with this class. After this, the instance variable s associated with `FourInt` is assigned the value d. As usual, this constructor code is executed after the 'empty' object is created and any explicit initialization is performed.

The invocation of the superclass constructor can be done only as the *first statement* of the enclosing constructor, to ensure that all superclass data is correctly initialized, following the three-step procedure outlined earlier.

Default use of superclass constructors

You may wonder at this point: what would happen if you did not explicitly invoke the superclass constructor? How would the superclass data be initialized?

The answer is that if you do not call a superclass constructor, Java will call it for you by default. The only superclass constructor it makes sense to call by default is a zero-argument one.

We can now state what the default constructor contains. The default constructor for every class `ClassName` (other than `Object`) looks like this:

```
public ClassName ()
{
    super();
}
```

When this constructor is invoked, the first two steps of the construction process take place and then the superclass constructor is invoked. The superclass constructor is subject to the same rules. This results in any instance variables that have not been explicitly initialized having default values.

Only the class `Object`, which is at the top of the class hierarchy, does not call a superclass constructor, because it has no superclass.

If you invoke a superclass constructor explicitly, you are able to take better control over the initialization of the variables defined in the superclass.

4.6 Garbage collection

We have seen a lot about how we create new objects. The converse question is: how do we get rid of them? If objects simply continued to exist once created, it is quite possible that we would run out of memory.

When an object is created, the Java interpreter will create enough space for it to exist, including enough memory for its instance variables. When an object is no longer in use, the system will destroy it and return the space allocated to the object to a reservoir of free memory.

For example, if you had a method as follows:

```
public void greetUser (String username)
{
    String greeting = "How do you do ";
    System.out.println(greeting + username + "?");
}
```

then the system would create space for the `String` object referenced by `greeting` to hold the characters in the string literal. When the method completes its processing, the space allocated to the object referenced by `greeting` will be marked as unused. This is safe to do because the reference is declared in the method, and it no longer exists outside the method. (It is a *local variable*.)

Periodically, the Java run-time system returns to the reservoir of free space all the memory that is occupied by unreferenced objects. This process is known as **garbage collection**.

Garbage collection can cause a program's execution to slow down, so you would probably not want it in a real-time system (for example, in an aeroplane fly-by-wire system). On the other hand, it is a much safer approach than relying on a programmer to decide when memory is free to be returned to the system, so in a general-purpose language such as Java it is seen as a good feature.

Some other languages, including C, leave garbage collection up to the programmer. This is often a source of subtle errors.

SAQ 5

(a) To what kind of data does the garbage collection facility apply?

(b) Give two examples of cases when the Java run-time system would feel it is safe to garbage collect an object.

ANSWERS ....

(a) Garbage collection applies only to objects.

(b) If all references to an object are out of scope, the space that the object occupies can be reclaimed.

It may also be the case that any reference variables that used to refer to the object have been made to refer to some other object, or have been set to the value `null`.

5 Some examples of Java classes

The aim of this section is to present some simple examples of classes in order to reinforce the ideas that we have described in the unit and show you how such classes are developed.

5.1 A car tracking system

Suppose that a navigation system needs to track the position of a car using measurements on a grid and to calculate a straight-line distance between positions of the car at different times. Our first example defines a class `CarTracker` for such an application. There are four instance variables, describing the car's starting and ending coordinates. This is shown in Figure 5, in which a car's position is described as a pair of numbers (x, y), with x increasing to the right, and y increasing to the top of the grid (coordinate) system.

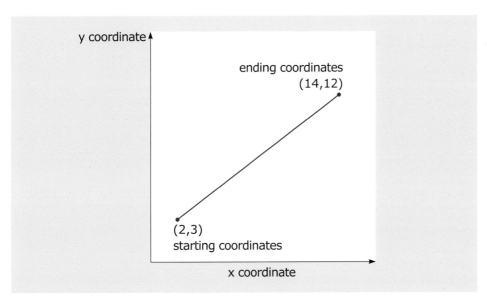

Figure 5   A grid system

We will require:

▶   a constructor that sets the starting and ending coordinate values;

▶   setter and getter methods for the four coordinate values;

▶   a method that returns the distance between the starting and ending points;

▶   a method that checks whether the distance between the starting and ending coordinates is greater than a specified distance, perhaps to decide whether the trip is short enough to make.

The code for this class is shown below:

```java
public class CarTracker
{
    private int startX, startY, finishX, finishY;

    // a four-argument constructor
    public CarTracker (int startXValue,
                       int startYValue,
                       int finishXValue,
                       int finishYValue)
    {
        startX = startXValue;
        startY = startYValue;
        finishX = finishXValue;
        finishY = finishYValue;
    }

    // setter methods
    public void setStartCoords (int newX, int newY)
    {
        startX = newX;
        startY = newY;
    }

    public void setFinishCoords (int newX, int newY)
    {
        finishX = newX;
        finishY = newY;
    }

    // getter methods
    public int getStartXValue ()
    {
        return startX;
    }

    public int getStartYValue ()
    {
        return startY;
    }

    public int getFinishXValue ()
    {
        return finishX;
    }

    public int getFinishYValue ()
    {
        return finishY;
    }
```

```
/* a method to find the distance between the starting and
ending points of the car's position */
public double journeyDistance ()
{
    return Math.sqrt(Math.pow(finishX - startX, 2.0) +
                    Math.pow(finishY - startY, 2.0));
}


/* a method to tell if the distance between starting and
ending points of coordinate positions is greater than a
specified length    */
public boolean greaterThan (double distance)
{
    return (journeyDistance() > distance);
}
}
```

journeyDistance uses a standard formula that calculates the hypotenuse of a right-angled triangle.

Our `journeyDistance` method returns a `double` because we need to use `Math` class methods and they operate on and return `double` values.

An object invoking the `greaterThan` method will use its `journeyDistance` method to determine whether the journey distance is greater than the `distance` specified in the `greaterThan` method's argument.

Activity 3.2
Using the `CarTracker` class.

5.2 A security monitor

The second example forms part of the security system of the applet accessed by the `User` class. One of the major concerns of the developers of software for the internet is preventing illegal access to a system's resources and also identifying illegal access, when it happens, as quickly as possible.

How can a system determine that an intrusion has happened? One way is to take advantage of the fact that the vast majority of users of computer systems are people of habit. For example, one kind of user may access the applet in the early morning and log in three or four days a week. A sales clerk for a company may access a system only twice a day: in the morning and after lunchtime.

In order to determine whether a user is behaving in an unusual way, so that there is a possibility of impersonation by an intruder, applications can keep details of users' past activity. This data might include the date of last logging on, the number of accesses since the beginning of the month and the average number of accesses per day. A program known as a security monitor would scan through this data and display the identity of any users who were behaving out of character.

To keep the example simple, we will assume that only two items of data are kept: the time of last access to the system and the number of accesses made in the current day.

The security monitor class will require access to our class called `User`. We will modify the `User` class so that it has the extra instance variable for the time at which a user last accessed the system, which we will call `lastAccessTime` and (to keep the example simple) model it as an integer.

```java
public class User
{
    private int lastAccessTime;  // new instance variable
    private int numOfAccesses;
    private String userID;
    private String emailAddress;

    // constructors not shown

    // getter and setter method examples
    public String getUserID ()
    {
        return userID;
    }

    public int getNumOfAccesses ()
    {
        return numOfAccesses;
    }

    // new method to return last access time
    public int getLastAccessTime ()
    {
        return lastAccessTime;
    }

    public void updateNumOfAccesses ()
    {
        numOfAccesses++;
    }

    // new method to set lastAccessTime
    public void setLastAccessTime (int t)
    {
        lastAccessTime = t;
    }
}
```

We will call our security monitor class `SecurityRecord`. It will have an array of `User` references and two constructors: one to create a default-sized array, the other for a number of records specified by an argument.

A skeletal description of the class follows:

```
public class SecurityRecord
{

    private final int DEFAULT_RECORDS = 100;
    private User [] accessTable;
    private int numOfUsers;

    // a zero-argument constructor
    public SecurityRecord ()
    {
        numOfUsers = 0;
        accessTable = new User [DEFAULT_RECORDS] ;
    }

    // a one-argument constructor
    public SecurityRecord (int arraySize)
    {
        numOfUsers = 0;
        accessTable = new User [arraySize] ;
    }
    // code for other methods not shown

}
```

accessTable is an array of User references.

Let us assume that a number of methods are required:

▶ getAccessesForUser, which tells how often the user has accessed the applet, given a user ID;

▶ getLastAccessForUser, which tells the last time a user accessed the applet, given a user ID;

▶ logsOn, which records a login for a user, given a userID and time;

▶ addUser, which adds a new user to the accessTable array.

We will make use of a helper method, findIndex, which returns the index at which an identified user's security data is stored in the SecurityRecord object's array of users.

The code for the addUser method is shown below. All it does is add the new user reference to the end of the array holding user references and increment the total number of users. This method assumes that there is room to add the user.

```
public void addUser (User us)
{
    accessTable [numOfUsers] = us;
    numOfUsers++;
}
```

To illustrate the structure of a SecurityRecord, suppose that we created an object of this class, referenced by security, as follows:

```
security = new SecurityRecord(4) ;
```

This allows room for just four users in the security record. Suppose we then add two users to the security record, by invoking the addUser method on the object referenced by security twice.

Figure 6 clarifies the structure we have created. An object of class `SecurityRecord` is referenced by `security`. The `SecurityRecord` object has a reference to an array of `User` references. The first two references in the array object have been initialized so that they point at `User` objects. The details of objects of class `User` are not shown, but they would have the four variables shown in the definition of `User` above: namely, integer variables `lastAccessTime` and `numOfAccesses`, and `String` variables `userID` and `emailAddress`.

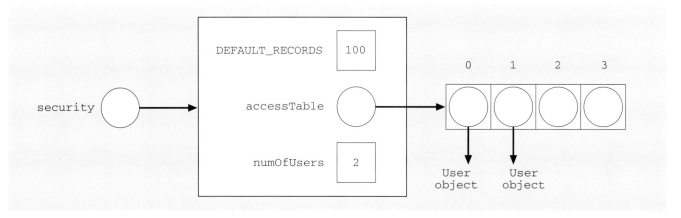

Figure 6   The **SecurityRecord** object referenced by **security**, after two users have been added to the record

We now show the code for the remaining methods of class `SecurityRecord`.

The code for `logsOn` is shown below, with the user's ID passed as a string argument:

```
public void logsOn (String id, int time)
{
    int index;    // to store the accessTable user location
    User u;       // for local use only

    // use the helper method to find the user's index
    index = findIndex(id);

    // store a User reference to make code easier to read
    u = accessTable[index];

    // set this user's lastAccessTime
    u.setLastAccessTime(time);

    // increment this user's number of accesses
    u.updateNumOfAccesses();
}
```

The code for the method that returns the number of accesses a user has made, given the user's identity, is shown below:

```
public int getAccessesForUser (String id)
{
    int index;   // location of the user in the accessTable
    User u;      // for local use only

    // use helper method to find user's index
    index = findIndex (id);

    // store a reference to the user
    u = accessTable [index];
    return u.getNumOfAccesses ();
}
```

The code for the method that returns the time of last access is shown below. It is similar to getAccessesForUser, but we have combined the first two steps:

```
public int getLastAccessForUser (String id)
{
    User u;

    // findIndex is used directly to determine index of
    // user in array
    u = accessTable [findIndex (id)];
    return u.getLastAccessTime ();
}
```

In fact, we could have combined all the steps as follows:

```
public int getLastAccessForUser (String id)
{
    return accessTable [findIndex (id)].getLastAccessTime ();
}
```

However, we prefer to show some intermediate steps to make code easier to read.

The final method is the private helper method findIndex, which finds a specified user within the accessTable, making use of the equals method defined for strings. Our methods using findIndex have assumed that a user is always found, on the basis that we are just giving an example and wish to keep the code as simple as possible. Later we shall see other ways of dealing with issues like this.

```
// return the index of the identified user in the accessTable
private int findIndex (String id)
{
    int i = 0;
    User u;
    while (i < numOfUsers)
    {
        u = accessTable [i];
        if (u.getUserID ().equals (id))
        {
            return i; // return the user's index
        }
        i++; // try the next index
    }
    return -1;
}
```

The findIndex method is defined as private since it reveals information about how the security records are stored and clients of this class do not need access to this information. This gives the full definition of the SecurityRecord class as:

```java
public class SecurityRecord
{
    private final int DEFAULT_RECORDS = 100;
    private User[] accessTable;
    private int numOfUsers;

    // a zero-argument constructor, creating a default size record
    public SecurityRecord ()
    {
        numOfUsers = 0;
        accessTable = new User[DEFAULT_RECORDS];
    }

    // a one-argument constructor
    public SecurityRecord (int arraySize)
    {
        numOfUsers = 0;
        accessTable = new User[arraySize] ;
    }

    public int getAccessesForUser (String id)
    {
        // use helper to find user's index
        int index = findIndex(id);
        User u = accessTable[index];
        return u.getNumOfAccesses();
    }

    public int getLastAccessForUser (String id)
    {
        int index;
        User u;

        // use helper to find user's index
        index = findIndex(id);

        u = accessTable[index] ;
        return u.getLastAccessTime();
    }

    public void logsOn (String id, int time)
    {
        int index;
        User u;

        index = findIndex(id);

        // store a reference to make code easier to read
        u = accessTable[index] ;

        // set this user's lastAccessTime
        u.setLastAccessTime(time);
```

```
        // increment this user's number of accesses
        u.updateNumOfAccesses();
    }

    public void addUser (User us)
    {
        accessTable[numOfUsers] = us;
        numOfUsers++;
    }

    // return the index of user with userID id
    private int findIndex (String id)
    {
        int i = 0;
        User u;
        while (i < numOfUsers)
        {
            u = accessTable[i];
            if (u.getUserID().equals(id))
            {
                return i; // return the user's index
            }
            i++; // try the next index
        }
        return -1;
    }
} // end of class SecurityRecord
```

6 Inheritance revisited

Inheritance is a key property of Java and other object-oriented programming languages. Used wisely, it enables the programmer to reuse large amounts of software – not only software that he or she has written, but also software in the Java class library. In this section we discuss some of the ways Java deals with reuse of the data members and methods of inherited classes.

6.1 Extending the `User` class

As an example, let us say that we have developed a number of applications using our `User` class, but that we now want to differentiate between normal users and 'privileged' users. The former will be allowed to access some of the facilities of the application; the latter will be able to access all the facilities of the application but will need to pay for the privilege. Privileged users have all of the attributes of normal users, and some additional ones.

Since privileged users will still require the instance variables and methods associated with ordinary users, we can develop a new class called `PrivilegedUser` that inherits from `User`. We can continue to use the `User` class alongside the `PrivilegedUser` class. In order to cater for the privileged users we will need to provide them with a password, to prevent other users accessing their facilities.

```java
public class PrivilegedUser extends User
{
    // additional instance variables
    // for example, a string password
    private String password;

    // methods for a privileged user
    // for example, a method that
    // changes a privileged user's password.
    public void setPassword ()
    {
        // some code that sets password
    }
}
```

If we have developed the `User` class following the principles of information hiding, we will not need to know the details of how `User` achieves its work; we can simply get on with writing `PrivilegedUser`.

The relationship between the two classes allows us to say that an object of the `PrivilegedUser` class **is-a** `User` object. By this, we mean that any methods we can invoke on a `User` object can be invoked on a `PrivilegedUser` object, subject to the access modifiers of the class allowing it. For example, a `PrivilegedUser` object can make use of the `User` method `getEmailAddress` because that method is inherited.

We draw such a relationship as illustrated in Figure 7, with the inheriting class below its superclass and connected to its superclass with an open-headed arrow.

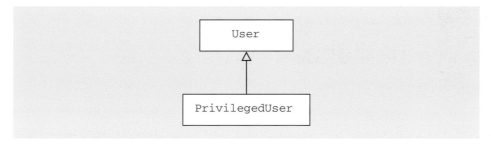

Figure 7 The **PrivilegedUser** class inherits from the **User** class

You may think of a PrivilegedUser object as a User object, depending on which is more convenient.

On the other hand, a User object cannot do the work of a PrivilegedUser object, because a User object does not have all the instance variables or methods that a PrivilegedUser has.

If you keep in mind this relationship between a subclass and its superclass you will be able to understand when casting and assignment between reference types are legal.

6.2 Reference casting and assignment

It is always legal to assign a reference of a subclass type to a superclass type. For example, it is legal to write:

```
PrivilegedUser p;
User u;
p = new PrivilegedUser();
u = p; // legal without a cast
```

This is similar to promotion with primitive types, where a primitive variable is automatically converted to another primitive type. In this case, there is an automatic conversion from the PrivilegedUser reference type to the User reference type. This kind of automatic conversion only occurs from a subclass type to a superclass type. As we said earlier, a PrivilegedUser 'is-a' User (by inheritance) so this conversion makes sense.

Casting a subclass type to a superclass type

Reference types can be cast using the same mechanism as for primitive types: the desired type is put in parentheses in front of the expression whose type is to be changed.

For example, the assignment shown previously can be written using a cast as follows:

```
u = (User) p; // explicit cast to type User
```

This makes explicit that u will reference a different type of object. This cast is not required, however, because a PrivilegedUser object is a User already, by inheritance.

So, after this assignment, with or without a cast, the User reference u is referring to a PrivilegedUser object. This is safe because any method you invoke on a User can also be invoked on a PrivilegedUser. So in fact, a User reference could reference either a User or a PrivilegedUser kind of object.

This is a general principle: a reference can refer to an object of its type, or to an object of any type below it in a class hierarchy, without the need for a cast.

Casting a superclass type to a subclass type

Another general principle is that it is not allowed for a reference to refer to a superclass type object. This means that it is not legal to write the following assignment statement:

```
p = u; // u could reference a User or PrivilegedUser object!
```

Why not? We cannot allow assignment of a `User` object reference to `p` because a `User` object has no `password` variable or `setPassword` method. If `p` references a `User` object, the `setPassword` method cannot be invoked on `p`.

In general, we cannot allow this kind of assignment because we will no longer know what methods can be invoked on the referenced object.

However, notice that the `User` reference `u` could in fact refer to a `PrivilegedUser` object.

Therefore, if we have additional information and are convinced that the assignment will work, we can inform the system using the usual cast mechanism as follows:

```
p = (PrivilegedUser) u;     // cast required for this assignment
```

The compiler will accept this, on the assumption that we have thought through the implications. Any problems with this assignment cannot be detected until the program is actually running. If `u` is referencing a `PrivilegedUser` object, this will not cause any problems at run time and we will be able to invoke all the `PrivilegedUser` methods on the object referenced by `p`. However, if our reasoning was incorrect, and `u` is referencing a `User` object, this assignment would cause your program to crash with what is known as a `ClassCastException`.

There is a mechanism for determining the type of object referenced by a variable, so that you can avoid crashing your program with this error.

The facility we have described here may seem troublesome, but in fact it allows you to write flexible code. This feature is discussed in *Unit 5*.

6.3 Overriding

One issue we have not discussed is what happens if a subclass redefines instance variables or methods that exist in its superclass. The redefining of instance variables is called **hiding** and the redefining of methods is called **overriding**.

We do not typically want to hide variables by redefining them in a subclass, because it is best to keep the way data is stored uniform, as far as possible, and to avoid duplication of data.

On the other hand, it is common that you want to use the same name for a method in a subclass as the superclass, but have the behaviour be different in the subclass. There is no reason why two objects have to respond in the same way to a method invocation. This is referred to as overriding.

As an example, suppose that both our class `User` and its subclass `PrivilegedUser` have methods called `getUserID` with the same signatures. The superclass method returns the value of the `userID`, but the `PrivilegedUser` class method returns only a fixed string message:

```
public class User
{
    private String userID;

    public String getUserID ()
    {
        return userID;
    }

    public void setUserID (String id)
    {
        userID = id;
    }
}

public class PrivilegedUser extends User
{
    public String getUserID ()
    {
        return "name is secret";
    }
}
```

In this case, because the subclass method uses the same signature as the public superclass method, the subclass method is said to override the superclass method.

This should not be confused with overloading, in which a class has several methods with the same name but different argument lists.

If we wrote the code:

```
public class TestUser
{
    public static void main (String [] args)
    {
        // has User and PrivilegedUser references
        User u = new User ();
        PrivilegedUser p = new PrivilegedUser ();

        u.setUserID ("Emma");
        p.setUserID ("Kate");

        System.out.println (u.getUserID ());
        System.out.println (p.getUserID ());
    }
}
```

Then we can rely on the fact that the output is:

```
Emma
name is secret
```

The method that is invoked is determined by the type of the object it is invoked on and not by the type of the reference. The references `u` and `p` are referencing `User` and `PrivilegedUser` objects respectively, so the first invocation of `getUserID()` results in the execution of code defined in the `User` class, while the second invocation results in execution of code defined in the `PrivilegedUser` class.

This feature allows us to redefine the effect that certain methods have in a subclass, to suit the subclass. It also ensures that if we accidentally override a superclass method, the subclass behaviour will occur if the referenced object is of the subclass type. In other words, we always get the behaviour we intend for the object.

Here is another example of a situation in which we might want to reuse the same method name in subclass and superclass, but provide different behaviour. Suppose we have a `greeting` method:

```
public class Mother
{
    private String name;

    public String greeting ()
    {
        return "Pleased to meet you";
    }
}

public class Child extends Mother
{
    public String greeting ()
    {
        return "How's it going? ";
    }
}
```

You can see that it is quite reasonable that superclass and subclass have different behaviour for the same method, as it is quite natural for each to respond in their own way to invocation of the `greeting` method.

It is useful that the two classes `Mother` and `Child` above 'speak the same language' in the sense that objects of these classes can have the same methods invoked on them. This is one way in which object-oriented programs achieve reuse of code. If it were necessary to have different names for the greeting method in `Mother` and `Child`, our code would have to provide different pathways for dealing with these kinds of objects.

This is known as polymorphism. It is discussed in detail in *Unit 5*.

As things stand, we can write a single method to invoke a method on both `Mother` and `Child` objects. For example:

```
public void hello (Mother m)
{
    System.out.println (m.greeting ());
}
```

The `hello` method can receive either a `Mother` or a `Child` reference as an actual argument. If it receives a `Child` reference, an automatic cast to the superclass type will take place. The type of the object referenced by `m` will then determine the observed output.

Inheritance and overridden methods

Overridden methods are not inherited. That is, they cannot be invoked using their simple names.

In the example shown, because `User`'s `getUserID` method is `public`, it would normally be accessible using its simple name in the subclass. However, in this case it is not accessible using the notation `getUserID()` because that refers to the method of the same name defined in `PrivilegedUser`.

You can use the keyword `super` as a reference to a superclass. If the subclass needed to make use of the superclass `getUserID` method, it could do so by invoking `super.getUserId()`. This is allowed because that method is `public`, so it is accessible. The word `super` does not allow you to break information hiding.

Only a subclass can invoke the superclass method in this way. For example, `PrivilegedUser` could have the code:

```
public String getUserID ()
{
    return super.getUserID() + " name is secret";
}
```

SAQ 6

Given the following code, what output would you expect?

```
public class Parent
{
    public void method (int i)
    {
        System.out.println ("Parent " + i);
    }
}

public class Child extends Parent
{
    public void method (int i)
    {
        System.out.println ("child " + i * 2);
    }
}
public class TestChildParent
{
    public static void main (String [] args)
    {
        Parent q = new Child ();
        Parent p = new Parent ();
        Child c = new Child ();
        c.method (1);
        p.method (2);
        q.method (3);
    }
}
```

ANSWER...
```
child 2
Parent 2
child 6
```

The class hierarchy

Before looking at how we can develop more classes of wider use in later units, we need to understand the idea of the inheritance hierarchy, which we briefly introduced in *Unit 1*. This section further explores the Java inheritance hierarchy and two of the methods that are common to all classes.

7.1 Java inheritance hierarchy

You will remember that we described inheritance and a graphical notation that describes the inheritance hierarchy. An example of this notation is shown in Figure 8. This shows `classC` and `classD` inheriting from `classB` which, in turn, inherits from `classA`.

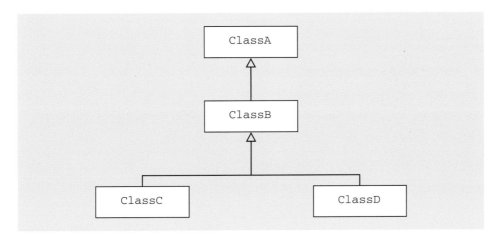

Figure 8   An inheritance hierarchy

All the classes in Java form part of a massive inheritance hierarchy. There will be two types of class in this hierarchy: user-defined and those within the Java class library. Later we shall look at many of the facilities within this library – all that you need to know at this stage is that it consists of a large number of classes, which are useful for a variety of application areas.

Figure 9 shows part of the Java inheritance hierarchy, including the root of the hierarchy, which is the class whose name is `Object`. The class `Object` has no superclass.

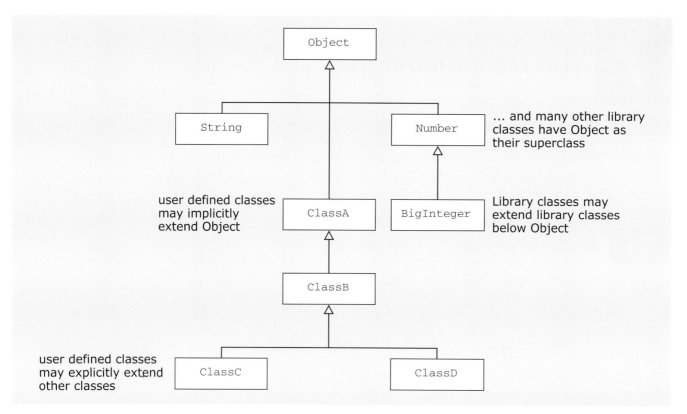

Figure 9   Part of the Java inheritance hierarchy

The classes that programmers develop will:

▶   either explicitly inherit from some named class by using the keyword extends;

▶   or implicitly inherit from the class whose name is Object.

As an example of this, consider the declaration:

```
public class ClassName
{
    // instance variables
    // constructors
    // methods
}
```

Even though this class does not include the keyword extends, which would indicate that the class inherits from another class, Java assumes that it will inherit from the class known as Object. It would mean the same thing if we wrote:

```
public class ClassName extends Object
{
    // instance variables
    // constructors
    // methods
}
```

So every class extends another class, except for the class Object, which is at the top of the class hierarchy.

You will see in *Unit 5* that having the superclass Object at the top of the class hierarchy enables us to develop very powerful classes. It is also important because Object has some significant general-purpose methods. Key amongst these are equals, clone, toString and finalize. We will consider only toString and equals here. These methods are inherited by every class (other than Object, which defines them).

7.2 The `equals` method

Every object in Java has a method whose name is `equals`. The reason is that `Object` has a public method of this name and every class inherits from `Object`, either directly or indirectly. The header for this method is as follows:

```
public boolean equals(Object obj)
```

However, `Object`'s implementation of `equals` returns `true` if its `Object` type argument is the same reference as the receiver object reference. So the inherited `equals` method returns `true` if the argument to `equals` has the same reference as the object on which this method is invoked.

This method is provided so that all objects can respond to an invocation of an `equals` method, but it is expected that programmers will override this method so that its behaviour makes sense for its class.

When performing tests for equality of two objects, you must remember that a reference is not an object, and a reference value (presuming it is not `null`) represents the location of an object in memory. Comparing two references for equality does not compare the contents of the objects referenced. This is why, if we need to compare objects of a class, it is necessary to write a method.

We will take the `User` class as an example.

We originally defined objects of the class `User` to have three instance variables: a string representing a user ID, a string representing an email address, and an integer representing a number of accesses.

We wrote a two-argument constructor to initialize the data:

```
public User (String anID, String anAddress)
{
    numOfAccesses = 0;
    userID = anID;
    emailAddress = anAddress;
}
```

When we write the code:

```
User emma = new User("Cornes", "cornee@joke.com");
User maria = new User("Cornes", "oranje@holland.com");
```

we create two `User` references and two `User` objects. These objects in turn contain references to `String` objects. A picture of the object referenced by `emma` is shown in Figure 10.

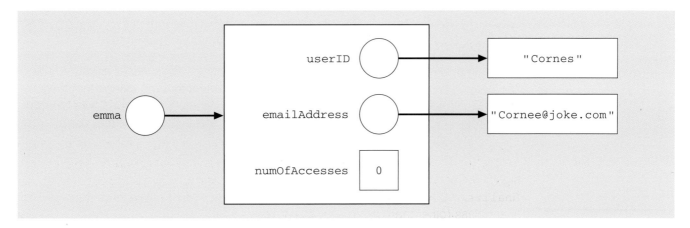

Figure 10   The reference **emma** and the object referenced by **emma**

Consider what happens when we do the following test:

```
if (emma == maria)
{
    System.out.println("Same user");
}
else
{
    System.out.println("Different user");
}
```

The output of this piece of code would be "Different user". This is not because the objects referenced by emma and maria contain different data (although they do), but because the test compares only the values stored in the references for equality, not the values stored in the objects referenced.

At some point we might write:

```
maria = emma;
```

This would copy the reference stored in emma to the reference variable maria. In this case, the output of the if statement would be "Same user" because the value stored in each of these references is now the same. (The object formerly referenced by maria might be garbage collected.)

Writing an **equals** method for the **User** class

In this section we show how you can write a method to compare the contents of two objects for equality.

For example, if we wanted to test for equality of User objects, we would write an equals method within the User class. (Because it is within the User class, the method can access the instance variables directly.)

Normally we would want to carry out an item-by-item comparison of the instance data of each object:

```
public boolean equals (User u)
{
    return userID.equals(u.userID) &&
           emailAddress.equals(u.emailAddress) &&
           numOfAccesses == u.numOfAccesses;
}
```

This method receives a User reference u as an argument, and compares the data in the object referenced by u with that in the User object in which this method was invoked. For example, numOfAccesses == u.numOfAccesses compares the values of the numOfAccesses variables in the object whose equals method has been invoked (hence we do not need to use a dot notation for its numOfAccesses instance variable) with the numOfAccesses value in the object referenced by u.

Notice that we had to use the equals method of the String class to compare the contents of the string instance variables. We want to test that the strings that these variables reference are the same. (If we had written userID == u.userID, for example, the condition would be that the references userID and u.userID are equal.)

The results of the three tests in the `equals` method for the objects `maria` and `emma` are shown in Table 1.

Table 1 Tests in the **equals** method for **emma** and **maria**

Test	Value	Comments
`userID.equals(u.userID)`	true	both have the value "Cornes"
`emailAddress.equals (u.emailAddress)`	false	the email addresses have different characters
`numOfAccesses == u.numOfAccesses`	true	both are 0

We could write either of the following to test equality of the objects referenced by `emma` and `maria`:

```
emma.equals(maria)
maria.equals(emma)
```

These two statements would have the same effect, although they would be invoked on different objects.

Notice also that when you write an `equals` method, it is up to you to decide which contents to compare for equality. You might have wished only to do the following, for example:

```
public boolean equals (User u)
{
    return userID.equals(u.userID);
}
```

So the behaviour of `equals` methods we write is whatever we consider to be sufficient to determine that two objects of a class are equal.

However, the examples we have shown above are both deficient in an important way and this is explained below.

Overloading versus overriding `equals`

The examples we have shown above are ways to overload, not override, the `equals` method because they have a `User` reference as an argument, whereas the inherited `equals` method has an `Object` as an argument. In order to override `equals`, we would have to write a method with the same signature as the method inherited from the class `Object`.

This is a significant point because other classes make use of the `equals` method whose argument is an `Object`, and if they are to behave correctly with classes you write, you must override `equals`. If you do not, other classes will continue to make use of the inherited `equals` method, which only compares object references for equality, not contents.

An example of a method to override `equals` in `User` is shown below.

```
public boolean equals (Object o)
{
    // cast the Object argument to a User type
    User u = (User) o;
    return userID.equals(u.userID) &&
            emailAddress.equals(u.emailAddress) &&
            numOfAccesses == u.numOfAccesses;
}
```

Here we have to cast the argument o from Object to a User reference before it can be used. This is safe provided that the method is passed a User type reference when it is invoked. You will see later that there is a way to test the class of a reference so that you can avoid a possible class cast exception in this kind of code.

SAQ 7

Is the cast User u = (User) o shown above casting up or down the inheritance hierarchy? Explain.

ANSWER...

This is a cast down the inheritance hierarchy from Object, which is the top of the hierarchy, to User, which implicitly extends Object. This is why it is not a safe cast.

7.3   The toString method

Another method that all classes inherit from Object is the toString method. The purpose of this method is to produce a readable text representation of an object's contents. The method has the signature:

```
public String toString()
```

The method that you inherit from Object produces the name of the class followed, after an @ symbol, by a numeric (hexadecimal) value computed using the object.

The exception is that the literal null or any reference whose value is null is printed as follows:

```
null
```

This is unfortunately indistinguishable in printed form from the string "null", although that is completely different.

For example, making use of a two-argument User constructor:

```
public User(String anID, String anAddress)
{
    numOfAccesses = 0;
    userID = anID;
    emailAddress = anAddress;
}
```

you might have written:

```
User a = new User("Tembo", "zamby@lusaka.zm");
System.out.println(a.toString());
```

The output would look something like this:

```
User@3fbdb0
```

Activity 3.3
Writing a toString method.

Activity 3.4
Putting it all together.

This is not very useful output, although it does identify the class of the object whose toString method we invoked.

In fact, it is not necessary to call the toString method in this context, as one version of the println method will attempt to convert its arguments to strings using their toString methods in any case. So you could have written:

```
System.out.println(a);
```

with the same effect.

If we want to have a particular form of output for our `User` objects, we can define a `toString` method in the `User` class. It might look something like this:

```
public String toString ()
{
    return "User " + userID + ", Email " + emailAddress;
}
```

Now:

```
User a = new User ("Tembo", "zamby@lusaka.zm");
System.out.println (a);
```

produces the output:

```
User Tembo, Email zamby@lusaka.zm
```

The `equals` and `toString` methods are both worth implementing for almost any class you write. The behaviour of the methods is up to you: you decide what makes two objects of a class equal and you decide what kind of text output you would like your objects to produce when printed.

Activity 3.5
Using an array of a reference type.

Activity 3.6
Writing a subclass that overrides a superclass method.

8 Summary

In terms of Java programming, this has been the most important unit of the course that you have read so far. It has described the facilities in Java for defining classes and also extending classes by means of inheritance.

We discussed an important principle underlying object-oriented programming: information hiding. This allows us to hide some of the details of how data is stored, and to write methods to manipulate data only under well-specified circumstances. We discussed the access modifiers that enable us to do this.

When defining classes, we are able to specify the starting state of objects when they are created through constructors. We discussed that it is possible to define several constructors for a class, the role of the default constructor, and how to use constructors when classes are inherited.

We have seen examples of overriding, which is the practice of redefining a method in a subclass such that the method in the subclass will have its behaviour adapted to that subclass. This is common practice in object-oriented programming and encourages software reuse.

In Java, all classes ultimately inherit from `Object`, which is the root of what is known as the Java class hierarchy. The advantage of this inheritance structure is that there exist a number of methods that can be invoked on all Java objects.

This unit forms the core of your Java knowledge and the ideas in it will be used time and time again in developing useful programs.

After studying this unit, you should be able to:

► implement classes in which you have specified the access level of methods and instance variables;

► understand the difference between instance variables and class variables, and be able to decide when to use each;

► write constructors for classes;

► use inheritance to develop new classes;

► discuss the nature of the Java class hierarchy and the purpose of the `Object` class as the root of this hierarchy;

► write an `equals` method for a class;

► write a `toString` method for a class.

Concepts

The following concepts have been introduced in this unit:

access modifier, class, class definition, class header, class method, class type, class variable, construct, construction, constructor, default access, default constructor, `equals`, garbage collection, getter method, helper method, `import`, information hiding, inheritance, inherited, Java class hierarchy, member, object construction, overloading, overriding, package, qualified name, reference type, reference variable, separation of concerns, setter method, simple name, static method, static variable.

Index